poets afloat

an anthology of canal poetry
edited by Mi...

first published 2019

Gert Macky Books

4 Cotham Vale
Bristol
BS6 6HR
drusilla.marland@gmail.com

copyright of all poems rests with their authors

cover design Dru Marland
illustrations Dru Marland, Audrey Nailor

ISBN 978-0-9926783-4-0

The Shift   Audrey Nailor

This is the world that's left when snow lets go.
Underneath were all these things;
The things we lost three months ago,
The things we thought had given up,
The things we thought we had let go.
Dawn's too long in coming, light too slow;
It's stuck in higher hills. Summer's sleeping under us
Waiting for her cue. Someone has to go -
The seasons don't just start, you know.
Something has to slip the catch;
Someone has to go and fetch
The summer from below.
These days it must be done by hand,
Tell the tamed and battered land
It's time to put aside the snow.
These things don't just get done, you know.
Things wait, the land half-bare,
And torn where it is bare,
While we argue and decide, breath steaming,
Someone lights a prayer, someone
Jokes of global warming.
Whose turn now for undercroft,
To hold the little torch aloft
To read the signs of warning?
To reboot the engine annual,
Who will go where summer sleeps,
Where resting spiders slithe and creep,
To set the heat to "manual" ?
Shabby now, with muddy boots
And trembling hands half-curved with cold,
(We ask: when did our hands get old?)
We spare a kick for manifold,
Flick the switch that turns the lights back on
and draws across the halcyon
The first pale flash of gold.

Needlework Christine Rigden

Winter-cold and snow-bright
light, diffuse and pale.
Bleached cotton fields
are quilted,
hedgerows and trees
appliqued.
Darting birds
(the final touch)
add their embroidery.

Midwinter Jinny Peberday

We awake to fields of white,
ice crystals hang from every leaf
the wind it blows with an edge of spite.
the birds have flown, have taken the light
for winter is a skulking thief
and we awake to fields of white
from our warm bed, a beautiful sight
but out in the fields there is no relief
from a wind that blows with malice and spite.
The world seems enchanted overnight
the wild wind snatches at every leaf
and we awake to fields of white
and leave our bed and soon our delight
is turned to stone, to disbelief
the wind it blows with an edge of spite
but still we have the lighting of fires, the Midwinter Rite,
the return of the Sun, the return of life
as it unfurls beneath fields of white
and a wind that blows with an edge of spite.

A Villanelle on Space   Georgina Beazeley

The boat is an ample ten foot wide, and fifty-seven long.
There's basic, boaty, boat stuff and the things I need the most
What shall I sing aboard my boat? A treasure-stasher's song?

A thick brown coat, and shoes of course and a bit-too-small-sarong
A ladle and a blender and a thing that makes the toast
Yes, the boat's an ample ten foot wide, and fifty-seven long.

I kept two friendly spinning wheels and my mother's trusty Spong -
A chest of beads, two teapots and my maps that show the coast.
What should I sing aboard my boat but a treasure-stasher's song

When tidied up, the table is just a small oblong
which gives me space to stash the trays to do a Sunday roast -
but the boat is only ten foot wide, and fifty-seven long.

There are shelves to stow my books on and a shiny breakfast gong
A dozen towels, some trinket-pots and a rack to put the post.
So what do I sing aboard my boat? Just a treasure-stasher's song

A sewing machine and serger, it really isn't wrong -
fabric crammed in boxes, piled above the sills - almost
Oh! the roof of the boat is ten foot wide, and fifty-seven long.
And all I sing aboard my boat is a treasure-stasher's song.

Rowde Pound   Fanny Gorman

Ice arms reach to hold hands
Strengthening contact across the pound
Patterns of thick oil brush strokes.
_____

Digits grip the hull in steadiness
Then throw up their limbs in abandon
Sliding over in chips and sheets.

The Stankie in Winter Emma Whitcombe

She struggles with the paths the world has chosen
Whatever valour dawns within her heart
The paths of ice are frozen and unfrozen

She is the water and the diver's cousin
She rails at glittering dragons where they dart
She struggles with the paths the world has chosen

She skates above the depths the lily grows in
Her feet make falling through a lazy art
The paths of ice are frozen and unfrozen

Damsels flock in summer by the dozen
They baffle, scatter, reconcile and part
She struggles with the paths the world has chosen

The heron furls and sails the wind that blows in
From northwards, where the hill displays the hart
The paths of ice are frozen and unfrozen

She cries towards the hill in brave percussion
Mourning light and calling off the dark
She struggles with the paths the world has chosen
The paths of ice are frozen and unfrozen

Mud Dru Marland

It is our medium of communication,
we wade through it, it clags our bikes
and is the topic of our conversation.
In the polite streets of towns we enter,
we hail each other at first sight
of clouty boots, dank hats, the scent
of woodsmoke that has browned and kippered us,
tallowing our clothes and coats
when skulking in the warmth of boats
that snugly through the winter skipper us.

Icebreaking Dru Marland

The frosted meadows glittered in the rising sun
and mallards walked on water laughing fit to bust
the day we broke the ice from Seend to Semington.

We stamped our feet, and let the engines run
to warm them up, as prudent people must,
and noticed frosty cows can also glitter in the sun.

Our bargepoles smashed the way - such fun!
to make our course out to the middle of the cut
and onward through the ice to Semington.

The moorhens who interrogated their reflections
were chased off by the sheets of ice we pushed
that rafted up, and glittered in the sun.

The prop clanked on the fragments now and then
and hulls were scoured of blacking, weeds and rust
by that infernal ice en route to Semington

And chastened, we agreed; all said and done
wise folk who like their boats stay put,
when meadows glitter in the sun
and ice is on the cut from Seend to Semingon.

Gannet Simon Kirby

That time a gannet thought he was a goose.
Lord knows how he arrived, but there he stood
at Little Bedwyn Lock, incongruous
amongst his friends, in desperate brotherhood.

Enjoy the waterways!   Jinny Peberday

(I found this poem lurking within the 23 pages of CRT's Licence Agreement
and a nature guide on their web pages)

We ask you to navigate in a bona fide manner
the Boat named and propelled by human
or animal force. Or the wind. And when we say
animal force, we don't mean dormice, of course,
since they hibernate from October to April
and this would impede your obligation to navigation.
Neither do we recommend that you harness stoats
or swans, since there is no evidence of compliance
in these species. And if your boat is propelled
by any or all of the four winds, your bona fide
navigation will certainly need to be in good faith,
you will require plenty of that. You must ensure
that there is a competent mallard on board
which must be fed on frozen peas. No toast.
No tuna sandwiches. You must not do
(or carelessly fail to do) damage or nuisance
to the delicious, soft, black fruit or squirrels
may dismantle or destroy the Boat named.
Are you a private individual? Do you leave footprints
in the mud? Do you intend for the Boat named
a purpose other than navigation? You must notify us
of these things in writing or with singing grasshoppers
in the summer months. Any person or heron
using the Boat, must be aware that Otters
can come aboard the Boat to affix
correspondence, contracts and court papers,
yellow flag irises and toads.

Timeo Danaos   Dru Marland
fragments of towpath conversations overheard from my boat

You're being a snob
I'll tell you that
an island on the Loire
you're being ungodly
and you're being like Lauren
she takes a lot of recreational drugs
like a lot
there's kids in her class
Trojan horse
Limonge
wasn't it Limonge?
we were going down the Danube
it was in France
there's kids in her class make £300
fifteen hours
I worked like a Trojan horse
down the Danube
what do you need a map for
it's a canal
before they go to school
in the morning
it was in France and
we were going down the Danube
Limonge
do people live on these boats
there ought to be
that's all that I can say
there ought to be rules and regulations
there are but
not one of these go to work
not one of them
Trojan horse
they're marginalised
because they haven't adapted to
the modern world

The Rat   Sarah Jean Bush

I know you abhor me, fear and despise
My very existence, it's there in your eyes.
There's food to be found for the next hungry brood.
I cannot be thwarted by your ugly mood.
Your scavenging ways leave rich pickings for me,
You will not find our nests so defiled.
You scatter and litter, and you don't see,
That you show no respect for the wild.
Your days are numbered as I watch and I fear.
The land bides it's time, and look; I'm still here...

Plank   Simon Kirby

Narrow plank, it takes a knack.
Bouncing is the worst, that weight
which on earth would dissipate,
resonates and bounces back.

Still Bitter   Audrey Nailor

The first time you fall into the canal
It honestly hardly seems fair,
The moment in balance of pure "fucking hell,"
The betrayal of that open air.
The worst thing about falling in the canal
Besides mud in your teeth and your hair,
Is the way that your pilot raises morale:
"Could you open the bridge while you're there?"

The Wanderer   Jinny Peberday
Paul Nash, 1911

One hundred years later
I follow you through that field,
the crops waist deep
the barley beards scratching at my skin.
The light, yellow and harsh
bleaching out memory.
This was the year you abandoned poetry.
I follow you into the trees, in search
of shade, of shadows and lost words.

This Boat   Michelle Smith
a song for boating parents to sing to their children

The bow is the pointy end, the stern is at the back,
the bollards keep you tied up safe, whether the tide be full or slack.
Port is on your left hand and starboard's on the right.
The tiller safely steers your craft through day and through darksome
night.
The hull is on the bottom, the coach roof is the top,
the gunwales run round the edge of the deck to save you from the drop.
The fo'c'sle holds the hempen ropes hung up and neatly coiled
the engine room holds the heart of the boat all greased and nicely
oiled.

Berries   Gail Foster

The berries in the hedge were red
And summer's dust was on the sloes
How soft she was, the old man said
To touch, her lips were berry red
How much I miss her in my bed
Her merriness, the scent of rose
The berries in the hedge were red
And summer's dust was on the sloes

Those conversations   Jinny Peberday

Those conversations
you only have with poets
about whether the light fades
or the darkness rises,
but whichever is true
it is dark.
The open doors let in the night
and the musty damp wood smell
of boaters' fires
and the hoo hoo of tawny owl, male,
with an answering wit! wit! wit! of the female.
Clouds obscure stars
hiding parts of constellations -
Orion's belt is missing a notch,
red Betelgeuse marks the hunter's shoulder
or is it his knee?
And there goes Cassiopeia
following her zigzag path.
I am watching the night
and watching for bats
and watching how my thoughts slow down
as I scatter these words across the page.

The Green Way Sarah Jean Bush

A quick check underfoot
Always the wrong shoes.
Drying crusts of mud,
Whorled and warped
By the shape of spring waters rush.
Leaf litter rustles, adrift
In the aged depression.
The elder lies snapped, fallen
Barring and breasting
The imperceptible way forward.
Woodpecker shrieks with laughter
As rooks barrel through branches
Dropping quills and twigs.
The needlesharp wind clips

The Unfit Take Flight Georgina Beazeley
an acrostic

Coming to the foot, you feel small - a hesitant mouse almost . . .
And away we go. The first is the worst
End not yet in sight but committed to.
Now and now and now our bodies bend to the task - take it easy
Ambitiousness is wasteful, conserve energy.
Negiotiating with our muscles is new - brave -
Dangerous to feel confident. Dangerous to feel tired.
All limbs. All muscles. Broken. Burnt.
But now it's not far. The lion's share behind. A bit left in the tank.
        A bit - just.
Last few gates. Breathe. Keep cranking. Pushing -
Eastward from Devizes.

Beardy   Dru Marland
an acrostic

Met him at Bradford while working the paddle
Idly appraising us, lips in a pout;
Surprised there's no man at the helm, just a rabble
Of women, he gave us a shout.
"Gor! Who's in charge of you all, then?" he blustered
(You know that we shouldn't be out on our own)
"No-one" said Chris, resolutely unflustered;
"It's teamwork" -and hopping on board, she was gone.
Sad little man, watching as we receded;
Tragically, nothing he had that we needed.

Charming my Trainers Before a Towpath Trawl
Michelle Smith

Hermes bless and make incredibly fleet
these swooshy second hand trainers
that chose to grace my feet.
Please repel the towpath mud
and those annoying little rocks
that always inexplicably,
get inside your bestest socks.
Please pick out the safest path
amongst the puddles and the dogs
and stick fast to slippery surfaces
and rise high above wind felled logs.
Please find a path that passes
folk that cheerfully wave and smile
and cushion my ageing joints
for mile after mile.

wunderthere   Audrey Nailor

A Pleiades poem, poorly translated from the minnow

wine-dark the water lowly
where flish (the we of us) is,
wait all-here somewhat sleepish
why yes this is how we fish thru
willow strandthru, o night river
whyever this is bed here, sleepling
with eyes-open, dreaming so we fish do..

Pero's Bridge   Deborah Harvey

It's early morning
Mist cuts loose the harbour's mooring
sets it floating over waters,
melting into sky

                     while I drop anchor in the present,
on this bridge of hearts and letters
marked on padlocks in scratches, Tippex,
permanent ink

                   It's not for me
to second-guess what you might think
if you could stand here on this crossing that is carrying
office workers, shoppers, lovers,
your slave name

                   but I'd seize
the hands of these couples, these children, I'd tell them
love knows nothing of shackles,
locks and keys

Chagall's violin   Jinny Peberday

Each stroke of the brush
a note of red or gold.
The solo violin improvises
with yellows and blues.
The child waits in the shadows
arms outstretched and empty
ready to gather up each silent song
while I stand with the listeners
frozen in time. Too late now
to learn to play like that -
unthought of for years
my violin
always more beautiful
when mute.

For Neil, on the occasion of the Devizes to Westminster Canoe Race   Gail Foster

I sit with Neil, and Neil with me
Beside ye old Devizes sea
Not seeing much go by at all
A few canoes, a tennis ball
A bird or two, a yellow petal
A dog, a jogger in fine fettle
Suspicious strangers full of bile
And nicer persons moved to smile

We're drinking coffee, Neil and me
And passing time companionably
I nearly drop my lens cap. Phew.
And Neil nearly drops his shoe
A fish goes plop, a water vole
("It's not a rat!") climbs in its hole
And Neil names the water's shade
As 'glim'. Hey word up, Neil, well played

The old canal, and Neil and me
So little and so much to see
So much to say, not much at all
I photograph the tennis ball
And Neil looking rather shy
As bits of twig and shit float by
Like time and stuff, we both agree
We're like so on it, Neil and me

The Bradford Flight Dru Marland

There's some wot dwells at Darlington
and some by Avoncliff
and they'll maybe jaunt to Diggers
if the swingbridge ain't too stiff.
And the fear of where they've never been
will haunt their dreams at night
for there's dragons beyond Lock 14
above the Bradford Flight.

And there's some wot braves the Kennet's floods
despite the gruesome tattle
'bout West End folk up to no good
and boats packed in like cattle.
And silent, high upon Caen Hill
they'll gaze with wild surmise
at the lowlands all before them still
and Wiltshire's farms and spires.
For there's adventures yet to come,
at Bowerhill and Semington;
but it's Lock 14 at Bradford,
yes, the Bradford Flight, in Bradford town
that's one lock up and one lock down
is gateway to the Shire!

Ripe for the Taking   Sarah Kitcatt

Bowl in hand, I head to the free fruit aisle
To plunder the overgrown hedgerow
Bejewelled with beady - eyed berries
It's that time of year for those in the know.
Tentative fingers seeking out
Weave their way through the thorny trap
A pull or a tug to test who's ripe
Staining my fingers with deep purple sap.
Some glint through a webbed shield
Others under guard of bracken and briar
Weighty clusters hang down low
But the juiciest, always a reach too far.
Truly, this bounty is worth the toil
I have rummaged and ransacked a plenty
My hitched pully and scratched forearms
Bare the scars from this foraging pantry.
Now to construct the most English of puds
A sought after treat at tea-time
Add apples and crumble and custard
The perfect partners in crime.

I Saw Three Ships   Ann Drysdale

Christmas on the canal. Three narrowboats
Remain along the bank. Fair-weather folk
Have battened down their hatches and gone home.
Tracy is still here, though, pushing her luck -
Haphazard hippie, ragtag water-gypsy,
At loggerheads with the authorities.
They want her off because she hasn't got
The proper papers, but the other boaties
Regard her with affection. Up she comes
Out of the cabin with her tie-dyed tee-shirt
Under her chin, tattooed arms cherishing
The little boy who suckles at her breast.
A voice calls cheerfully across the cut,
Tits out for the lads then, is it, Tracy?
Eff-off! she yells, with equal lack of malice.
The Perkins coughs and catches, comes to life
With the slow pulsing of a steady heart.
Tracy sets off towards the water-point,
Steering with one hand as the lordly bow
Crumples the cat-ice in its gentle progress
And baby Tom, snuggled in grubby fleece,
Nests in the safe curve of her other arm.
He's fallen fast asleep. The rose-hip nipple
Lies in the loose curl of his petal tongue.
His lips mime kisses and one dimpled hand
Adorns the bare breast like a living star.

My boat has…   Sarah Kitcatt

A swan's neck, yet no white feathers,
A fair old draught, but in all weathers,
A bulls-eye, but no darts or beer,
A rams head, but no fleece to shear,
A berth, but without the painful labour,
An uxter plate, but empty of flavour,
A bulkhead, but it's not fair of face,
A bow, but not one tied up with lace,
A buttie, but no jam or marmalade,
A fiddle, but one that cannot be played,
A taff rail, that is not very Welsh,
A windlass, that does not belch,
A pigeonbox, but never heard a coo,
Strange thing is though, my chimney flu!
A plank on which no pirates walked,
A thruster, at which everyone balked,
A tiller, but she won't give a penny,
A bank to moor, but bereft of money,
A stern, but it's really more a lampoon,
A gunwale, but thankfully no harpoon,
A cant, that most certainly can,
And no baby... but a well used pram!

Two Sonnets for Bridge 140   Gail Foster

I'm here again, up on the bridge, the one
Beside The Wharf, and cemetery gate
I come to watch the rising of the sun
Upon the water, and at noon, of late
To spot the river rat and dodge the cars
And even later, when the town's asleep
To stop to hear the owl, and see the stars
And cold Orion shimmer on the deep
I'm always here. It's odd, but even when
I'm elsewhere, I can close my eyes and see
The ways the seasons turn, and turn again
The ways of waves, and ravens in the tree
And me, above the water, as a ghost
Returned to haunt the place I love the most

This bridge. I blush, for long ago I had
A lover, and I kissed him here. And here
He wasn't mine to kiss, but I was bad
And it was Spring, and he was hot, and beer
Had made me wanton, as it always did
And both of us enamoured, by the drink
I blush, as I remember how we hid
Beneath the arch, and teetered on the brink
For almost half an hour. It wasn't good
Well, I was. He was rubbish, to be fair
I waited for the owl call from the wood
Nope. Nothing. I gave up and left him there
This bridge. I stop and blush, as I recall
The times I've come, and haven't come at all

We All Started With L Plates   Nordic Gerbil

If I had a quid for every time,
I've banged in a pin,
And secured a line,
On a drifting boat,
Which wasn't mine…
If I had a quid for each wet rope,
Thrown in my face,
By some poor dope,
Who was left with me,
As his very last hope…
If I had a quid for every cock,
Who I've helped out,
Coming into dock,
Or given a hand,
With their very first lock…
If I'd PAID a quid for what I never knew,
For everything,
Which I couldn't do,
Then I'd still be in debt.
And so would you…

Murmuration   Sarah Kitcatt

Magnificent dancers
move as one synchronised
mass. Shadows thick and thin.
Mesmerised, transfixed,
my sleighted eyes delight in
manoeuvers so deft. Ace
masters of telepathy.

Boater   Louise Tickner

The prophecy
of the Boater be
to live life
and live it free.

To live in tune with the water's song
And be at peace the whole day long
To remember to smile when it rains
And share in others' joys and pains.

Our little life on the waterways
Is a treasure to us and will be always.
The trees and the stars are the gifts we receive
And the sweet fresh air the joy we breathe.

Every day
we're blessed to be
in a world that only
the boaters see.

Semington Bridge   Georgina Beazeley

not the bridge with back arched

like a spitting cat which

blinds you as you climb

pass by the canal, the boats

and there the brook

where a bridge as

flat as Norfolk spans.

it was rebuilt - it says

raised letters on dull metal against stone

do not say why

the important thing it seems

is men (it was always men) strove

(they always strove) to mend it.

a person now, glancing down

a stranger, say

might think that laurel bowed

was dipping down in worship or to kiss

the water but

it is not so.

the flow is risen up

it reaches to embrace

or rather to engulf

and where the bough shrugs

off the rough advance

stars flung from water, bloom beside.

and still I do not know

the bridge rebuilt, for it says so

stone by stone, the stolid men

(with horses too to move the stone)

but before the men -

what then? What then?

Watching for the Swallows   Dru Marland

I'm by the bridge at Sells Green, to see the swallows come.
A boat called Foxhunter chugs past. It's an hour after dawn.
Score so far: one boat, and swallows none.

A cow clears its throat. The alpacas on the hill
graze in the lee of the hedge to ward off the chill.
The cockerel's crowing from the farm, as cockerels will.
Alpacas: seven. Swallows: nil.

The chiffchaff in the hedge behind me packs it in.
Oh, then it starts again. The woodpecker begins
to drum, then laughs. It's cold in this wind.
Bloody canada geese. Swallows? Not a thing.

A rush of song from an unseen wren.
The woodpecker does its impression of Sid James,
somewhere over there towards Rusty Lane.
Oh! The first blackcap! In the hedge there, then
answered from the llama field.Ten out of ten
For blackcaps! Swallows? Nowt again.

Stiff fingers. Going in. It's too bloody cold.
The sun looks like a dissolving aspirin. Two gold
-finches bob high over. Vapour trails have ruled
thin lines of shadow on the sheet of stratus cloud.
Blooming swallows. Shouldn't be allowed.

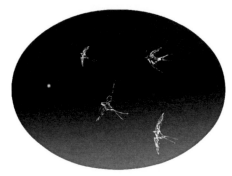

Storm   Jo Stait

The storm raged on.
The north winds blew
Rain in horizontal sheets
No sun shining through.
Saturated to the skin
Rain dripping off my nose.
Could do with webbed feet this morn
squelchy mud between my toes.
Storm rage on.
Howling through the trees
My jackets soaked through
And I've got muddy knees.
Storm passing over now
The air's beginning to clear
A show like that from the sky at night
Is not something to fear.
Some folk dont like lightning
Thunder claps too loud
Me I go outside n dance
Bare feet upon the ground.

The Heaven of Loved Steel Things   Audrey Nailor

In the Heaven that is set aside for all the loved steel things,
There are swords and ships and spacecraft, and a history of wings,
It is the final resting place for metal loved and named,
And no rust there doth corrupt, and there all time remains.

This is the hall of valour for the metal with a soul,
And in this endless hangar all that rusts has been made whole.
And they wait and take the form that they had when once loved best,
When polished, named and gendered - and in that shape they rest.

And that's where we will see her, when we find the open door,
For that final glance at what we loved before the final tour.
She will be there clear as daylight, small and bright among the hoard,
Between battleship and iron helm, twixt fighterplane and sword.

A narrowboat is nothing much, and among the greater craft
With her painted wooden panels, she will look half dear, half daft.
But we loved her like a lover and her soul was sweet as tea,
And she'll be there like we knew her, gentle Cleo Number Three.
.
And you could run your finger down the coachline bright as gold,
And if we step down to the engine, we'll forget that we've grown old.
All will be there as we left it, before babies, books and rust,
All will be there when we leave again, and shall not turn to dust.

All red and green and shining and as bright as wedding rings,
She'll be there, loved and lonely, in the heaven for steel things.
What is named will wait there, where all that rusted is made whole,
By virtue of their mettle, the metal with a soul.

Way to Go …   Ann Drysdale

"Edward"

My old boat will come back for me at the end.
The bitter stink of the coal-dust in its bilges
will carry the lost past like the sly cologne
of a long-ago lover.

Broken or sunken for so long, he will find it,
wring the black water out of its sodden timbers
and come for me with it, showing the stamp still wet
on his Skipper's ticket.

We will lie, Charon and I, on the roof of the cabin,
the tops of our heads hard against one another,
hands round each other's wrists holding the process
in a safe grip.

We will breathe, while our busy legs pedal together,
hobnails conjuring sparks from invisible brickwork,
legging our way through the echoing green-grown darkness
of the final tunnel.